The Braid

First Published: 2018
By TNC Press
This edition: 2021
ISBN: 978-1-9993715-3-1

https://williamcooke.net

The Braid
And Other Poems About Loss

William Cooke

TNC Press
2021

To Coming Home

'Nel mezzo del cammin di nostra vita
mi ritrovai per una selva oscura,
ché la diritta via era smarrita.

Ahi quanto a dir qual era è cosa dura
esta selva selvaggia e aspra e forte
che nel pensier rinova la paura!

Tant'è amara che poco è più morte;
ma per trattar del ben ch'i' vi trovai,
dirò de l'altre cose ch'i' v' ho scorte.

Io non so ben ridir com'i' v'intrai,
tant'era pien di sonno a quel punto
che la verace via abbandonai.'

The Braid

μοῖραν δ᾽ οὔ τινά φημι πεφυγμένον ἔμμεναι ἀνδρῶν,
οὐ κακὸν οὐδὲ μὲν ἐσθλόν. ἐπὴν τὰ πρῶτα γένηται...

...In that twilight, though, *something* was escaped!
A planet breaking from the well drawn path
Of the mathematical pencil tracing in an arc.
When tender tiredness
Spilled across me,
A road and trees
Around the rolling coffin—
Interred with the lame, in infamy,
I lie—
With the blind,
Milken cataract, an impacted iris
What opal moon reflects in my eye?

Day, then, was on us,
When I phased awake behind the dark and rolling glass.
The first fold of the valley
Thick fog on it,
Low down in the cloud and pines
We bump and glide,
In bocca al lupo,
Coniferous teeth,
Grey rock mane and
Cloud shag;
All it bearing down.
Through the field of horse and lance,
The surrealism of some ancient tussle,
Papists, Romans, Bonapartists
Lend us your swords,
Your horses and guns.
Lend your lives
Over the flat fields
Of Ceresole, Pollentia;
Montebruno and Tortona.
Or through the passes
Of those rigid alpine spines,
Whose morning fogs are soft.
Where the lull and still of all things,
Is false, in fact.
I'd seen your *città degradanti*
But not your natural state, old land.

I saw you inoculated with great black buboes
That hasten your death,
Saw you examined under halogenic whites,
Watched you draw in new blood
And sallow and sag;
Redden with fire until
Brown waste spread.
Though, that wisping cloud
Atop the pines
Is a vital sign—
Old things die slow
And are rejuvenated when,
To the truth,
They're given over.
Faded images repeat,
Fated for temporal hands
Every image must repeat.

In a strange bed,
But not a stranger's,
Held in white sheeted purgatory
Frayed as I around the edges,
Shedding like drowned or dead-in-water flesh—
What a skull I'll be one day,
Dry bone, no trace of brain
Nor my containing and limiting and carnal skin.
And, as every image must repeat,
What a procession of skulls I should be.
Whether we remember is something extra.
Least, if not to live again, we live in life again—
Where are we now, but in a recurrence of
Self-similar or modular beds?

The first storm breaks:
A romance arch on the rock mast arises from the dark,
Cracks the trees and lights against
The storming of the skies.
That, the tower, is the image in my mind
This Angel's tower, which watches down,
Has changed the taunting view behind.
And the walls of ancient rock
Have mutated the substance that surrounds.
Stores of grain ransacked, here
Fires that boiled men
A doctor's dark work I'm told,
A distant clinic, a dream

What kinds of story could be told of here?
In the stone yard,
What an unwinding she is
Of southern complexion—
As cloudfall descends
A flick of the falling, wine dark river—
After, she is blonde and bony;
Or with a miner's soft drawl;
Or breathy in her French;
Or otherwise;
Or an Australian one;
An American tongue;
Or something other again;
Another's wife? A mother?
How this mindlessness has made me numb!

While you are at home, love, little love, fading love, lost love,
Or at the house, I'd prefer to say,
Where you are disappearing physically and in me.

Red Miranda, so stranded!
I am in your dukedom,
And you are far.

But we have stumbled, both, alone, and in the dark
Midway in the forest of life. What waits ahead is fierce,
A slack maw, a brute stain, a sadness painted on the walls
In old woad or failed libido.
I have not thought of you in the refuge of the park,
Where we descend as a falcon's fading path,
A downward flight in turbulent motion.
In the histories and mysteries of older moments,
We are a tragedy creeping
That has crept since before we were found
On the sort of nondescript bed that bore our love.
You said to me once, 'I'm tired.'
Now it is a way of life,
A mantra, a simple sigh.
To return to you is pain,
To ever leave: the same.

Downwind other lives pass,
They live in the park
And smoke and wait
For something to save them.
Nothing will now nothing is left,
The heartwood is rot,
A structure stands for a fraction of its life;
The past begotten
Downward gyre. Vengeful Achaeans on the horizon
That stand to plunder all we built.

We are a series of stories,
Close in cause and content,
We are the singing soothed to silence,
The diminuendo of the cymbal crash,
Which birthed enough that we grew fat
And sick and weak, before we were even old.
Corrupted faces shaped by winds and tides,
Of profit beyond imaginations—
Tides that could not be turned by the gods aside;
Myth be made, and retold!

I was in one once,
I opened the Trojan gates;
The calm in the storm—
The rising stakes,
The staked heads.
I was always there,
Ten years away,
Penelope, in the shadow of
The Greek Sea,
I was the cursed wind
And the dragged man
And Circe's unchanged pig.
Ay, that's a tale! Replayed in the rock walls
Over a bottle of pinot and a regret and rue.
'I'm tired,' she said,
But in a difference sense.
One thousand faces,
Through a million faces,
I'd know her.

I'd know you.
Yes, the tale it twists and turns—
Descends and hurls me
Headlong into you,
Again; again—
I know you but I wish I knew you.

In this strange summer of reseeings;
Some short, some long,
Some longer than I could say,
I'd know you.
In those turning tides of time
I'd seek you out, though
I told you otherwise.
When did I know you first?
I fail to find.
The crescendo of the gyre, rolling
Turns in history,
Lost in the branches of my mind
Or lost in time—
What clued me off, whichever of my loves you be,
Was the black around your iris,
Clear of cataracts in the evening gloom
But more it was the lurking in the black rings
Behind all physical things, a tuft of eyebrow that has grown.
Your bitter substance that secretes a joke;
I laughed with you, on broken things, entirely free.

'Kick off your shoes weary one,
Returning wanderer kick off your shoes
Traveller who turns time,
Who repeats this historic day.'
I wonder: if not to turn the tides of time
But life—To rest a while on ravaged shores
For petty respite.
I wonder, if to turn the tide of life,
I'd've strength enough to find you resting too.
For strength it takes,
In this instant of decay
To submit oneself to lust and love
And unshackle from those chains.
The last time I know we loved,
The world around did fall.
Now it's on the rock again,
To the precipice we're called.

What a procession of skulls we've left behind us
And are us, what immortally named skulls we've been.
Famous things have tracked in our currents
And blessed our forking paths.
But still the state of now,
The descending state, inquiets me.
What worlds would shatter up
In the pregnancy of pasts?
I know at least one…

One rises, one falls
A moonsun
An eastwest
A lifedeath
A loveloss.
If I'd known all those things were at our hands,
To pierce across the sky as pinholes, or spill like milk,
I'd have been afraid,
But, Penelope: with her
I was small and safe.
Who am I this time?
In the face of one or other love
How many would submit
And bear for me a simple cycle, or
Entangle in the others?
Either/or
Neither/nor

The sun baked the earth in the summer,
Until the fog's fall.
The wisping cloud
Is a vital sign—
An endless thing never ends,
It merely circulates.
And, until the fog would break the heat,
We were safer underground
Or at night,
In the cold and damp
Of the chthonic walls.
That is, when earth would bring respite!
For the hot nights sometimes dragged out
And brought us all in sleep into pooling sweat.
And we stifled there, as a waxwork melts.
But when the dark rolled over the hills
(And after the rains)
When calm air blew, we were lead to distant hills.
We turned to the earthwork walls
Or the outside forests
With crawling roots
Clawing, and clutching
Our forms that sleep amongst the grit.
To stay, to sleep,
To rearrange opposing forces
Of nature and the schismed soul,
Captivated in the dreams
That replay and rework us all.

Under the nightlit tower of the Angels
My form, overthrown by herbs and weeds
And knotted into undergrowth,
Thatched into sleep forevermore—
There is peace! In the dark soil
Surrounded by the rain's smell
And herbs and weeds
With faint hints of mint or other worlds.

Wet earth and dry earth triune with me.
All oscillations in tune,
With me.

Tied to a wheel and tantalised,
I am rolled upon the wheel and down the hill,
Rolled into fields behind the hill
And into towns and down;
Into the dawn lit lake
And down.
I am racked upon the wheel and cycled,
Through all manner of mean lives to the bottom.

Sea scum and lake silt triune with me
All oscillations in tune,
With me.

What sailors here have drowned?
And seen from eyeless heads their clothes come ragged,
Have watched dilapidated hands grip and clench out
For the ropes of weeds
That tied and tore them
To stop the rise toward the light to die.

Dead men and live men triune with me
All possibilities, I am
Between.

Those fallen sailors with their blinded eyes, stay binded
When, on the wheel, I cut them free on my descent.
My lake is worse; it is of lava,
In which all manner of devils and darks are drownèd.
What widening worlds, of metaphysical significance
Lie beyond our growing reach!
Knowing nothing,
I am beneath,
In the realms of
Hades, senseless
In an Orphic sleep.

Old things die slow, you know?
And are rendered eternal
When given over to the grave.
Holy images of God's burning have
No power over the damp moss
Into which we long to be interred.
But the eternity of interment
That's a shallow shade!
And in the dark of perdition
Those sorry souls stay unsaved—

The one who lives
Is not the one the who loves.
Contrary to what the bookish think,
But the one who does.

The dying-and-rising one!
I pierce the sky
Reach the eternal high
Of the boundary that enshrouds our life.
I was born to be big,
Through the hundred lives I'd swallowed since
That nourished my weak and fleeting heart
To something tough—
To begin again, when
I'd sailed the wretched triremes,
Doctored plagues,
I'd turned the quickest silver
Into gold.
Then all in all,
When the weight was called
I heard the cadence of the dying fall
And fell from the heavens and fields of fools.
I found myself upon the tower tall,
A handful of manna, my only and all.
Creeping out of the crumbling walls:
I search my love again,
It is no longer pure.

I go home again,
And there I die anew.

A Poem for A Departure

I have watched you
Grow into your beauty
These six years—
And watched you flourish,
That it must be
You have placed steadfast roots;
Where mine are on the faltering rock,
Loose sand, or eroded soil,
Unsuited entirely to a life like yours.

I am a fickle force contained,
With cramping limbs
Longing to stretch over the rock face,
And I am worse yet:
A light, mercurial spirit
Shaking in the face of life
And drifting in dreamt seas,
Living falsehood and fancy.

Of late I have started to see you also stumble
On the dark path and the stone stair,
Which I have walked so many times
I know them eyeless.
Sometimes I wanted to watch you fall—
Like a parent watching the first turns
Of a creaking bike wheel.
What I wanted was to see you pick yourself up.

But merely I have caged you,
And rendered dark clouds around
And fixed them like grey stucco
To hold you in places you shouldn't be.
I, too, was bogged down there:
A jailer who wishes to fly free is no jailer at all;
He is as trapped as thee.

Untitled #1

Autumn's semi-gold brilliance
Steps through the haze,
As I hold her sweet, small frame.
And her bony shoulders
Become internalised.
Would we confess now
All the near misses,
I'd go well toward my grave!

Then hypotheticals come;
Lie ahead in blurry gaze
And bind my mind's diligence.
While Healing— The White Stag
Who dodged the crosshair—
Courses away in the moment
In which I'm ever transfixed
By the draw of the drink.

AN ELEGY, WRITTEN IN THE HUNDREDTH YEAR SINCE THE ARMISTICE

The stretched plain, the bare trees, the stark *gris*
Around Amiens, the day rains.
To have died in the rain
I do not know.
But carried on by small wheels
On wet roads, that
I know.

Over the bones of skinless trees,
Over the brown soil, so unforthgiving,
We roll with the hum of the car
In silence, pierced by a laugh or two,
An occasional jest, but other only Amiens.
By the light rain and slicks on the broken asphalt,
By that dismal day we go, into the cold.
Under grey cover,
The terrible place is opened before us,
A sombre land of lasts:
Last days and hours,
Last loves, and last chances.
Of last weeks before the bloom,
Last winters passed.

I know
That many of me came here to die.
Young men of the English ilk, that is,
Sloughed their skins and limbs,
Drowned beneath the mud.
They came for something we've long forgotten,
Yet arrived nonetheless in droves, like senseless cattle,
Their fates decided—
hands washed, in tides of battle.

Ah! For the country it was, or sold as such.
For the glory, carried on the wind
As far as the artillery thunder and
Long as it was not caught by the wire.

Whoever said, general or death,
'Je suis la tristesse du monde.'
The shared sadness, death is that—
la tristesse universelle.
Whoever spoke such things, he was right.
Death is the sadness of us all,
Where the great empire of life
Wishes only to ever grow,
It is a sadness that endures.

I had never seen a small church,
So buzzed with that electric *tristesse.*
Is a French death so other to me?
So other, when I see the landscape of my youth,
Reflected ersatz in the *terroir?*
Knowing that we all died here too,
A French death is not other to me, no.
It is just as potent, inducing sobs and cries,
The leaving behind, the respite,
The chilly pews and coat clad bearers;
Sober in dress.
None may see your face again,
Aside from in a dream,
Or on aging photo paper,
Whose colours leave;
Whose whites are already cream.
But you will be seen, again
Dispersed and free.
For a French death is as any other.
All are returned, their privileged moment leased and over.
A French death is not other,
I know.

I know
That *madame* lain before us,
She was good. She left a lasting legacy,
And was well loved; and loved well; and left those
Loved in health.
I wish the same for all life.
A French death is not other, no.

Nor are French folk in the throes of grief.
The sunlight splits the stained glass.
Relief from the cold air,
Respite, however brief.

To The Unelect in Valhalla

From the paradise of heathens, shrieking:
Land of welcoming arms, or arms—
The war dead, supplicated with a feast.
Those arms of warrior women
Fearful heights I dare not breach.

Cast out to wander awry, exposed surfaces,
Canyons baked, and folds of dirt and dry.
A sad cypress, rent in a wreath
Delivered down to me.
For the world tree is not our forebear's Ash,
But that sad cypress,
Hacked to death.
Or it is a yew,
From which my rebirth—
It grows out of me.

All who have seen the blood and peril—
Seen the daubings on the walls,
Turned around in cursive scripts,
On toppled alters, empty offices
Lit along a boiling sky—
And looked away;

And all who have aided butchers,
Supported the marauders and hoarders,
Opened gates to the plunderers;
Mongers of profit and usury who
Turn us out of our homes,
It is your time.

Untitled #2

I have gathered around me
Not despair, but demise;
The death of hope and all things thus.
Skeletal remembrances, circular spectres,
A blank page, shattered like a tombstone,
While I roam, with bitter water,
That fills my mortal matter.

Did I stray from the path of love? I did
Then I always returned with righteousness!
But you sinned
And transgressed, profaned our daily life
You died that day with a single sigh.
A lie, a turnaround
You fucked— I pray to pleasure.
For was the end worth every penny?
I guess not…
But your life's ship was not mine to steer
From the rocks and skrees
Yours was not my love to kill
And mine not yours.

I imagine:
He petted our cat and used our bed,
He culled our love in your willing wetness.
He awaited you and ate our food.
I don't know if you know what harm was dealt.
A falling rope was what I felt.
Then— I know it was you alone
Who were you?
A face I willed to destroy
Not for long…
A haze amongst settling ashes
A false face of lost promise
A grimace
An ugliness all along.

Then rage turns to ruefulness
A snaking path to newness, coiled
In the lost groves of carnivorous plants
Blocking the wide way home.
You were who you always were
But dimmed down and drowning
What would you give to take it back?
Or turn a page?
I hope I'll know.

Untitled #3

Broken, beaten
Damned, decayed
I traversed the motorway.
A second time
A third, I passed from you
That was the cost.

If he came banging on the door and pouring out with love
Would you let him cross?
A lie or not
Shrieking, persistent, mad with lust
Just as you want,
You would let him in...
Me: Moloch, I am a monster for you of ill repute
A screeching blazing brazen head aflame
An all devouring, burning womb
Where beaten boys are entombed.
A whoring out, a scraping out
A flushing of desire's fruit.
What little hurt is one fuck?
A torn wound, worthy sickness?
Ingrowing life, tumourlike?
The piercing buzzer
'Let's talk, lover,'
An unbolting latch,
A routed retreat
A loss of love
The final defeat.

Your slight tears are not what Moloch wishes.
But the bad blood of wretched sinners.
The red night, The red sands
The red light of red bronze.
I have demanded, life pays.
It's not so simple when your body belongs
To a jealous god's unreigned wrath and rage.

Is the anger too much?
It was always a lot.
You fall away, I fear
There is not enough sorrow,
Or water in the world for your tears,
That would let me let you back in.
The bridge between us collapsed one day.
Many perished,
I feared the road and way,
Back to the house in disarray.
Mountain passes, gripping seats
With misplaced anxiety.
Then everything changed.

The Crawling men

Wrapped in clothes of the wistful past,
I've lived and loved and now forgot
What each is like from pale city smog
That reaps its anger sevenfold.

Long I've wished that I could stand tall
In the city where ten thousand crawl.

Bawdry palaces under endless sky
Following streets equally unending,
Lined with the walls of realms exclusive
Where fires burn and madness rules.

I wish all men's lots cast to crawl
For if all men crawled then I could lord
Crown myself king of them all.

To place a curse of rag and bone;
To gasp and thrash in gutter pools;
To disinherit all I'll own.
Here comes the age of cursèd rule
When at last we all now crawl, into
My nights where dream takes flight.

Forever I wish that I'll stand tall
In that city where each soul crawls.

I've schemed to come along this path,
For the righteous one is straight and tough,
I've come as king of the crawling men
But they've clawed and gnawed and in due course
They've beat me down.

Oh how wrong I was to curse them all
Curse the empty, desperate souls to crawl.

Then when each man has had his day
Death's grimaced face is there to greet
Along the palaced roads, snowed in, lamp-lit
She's ever there (Don't try outwit) and,
As the man who trod his fellow down,
I'm cast as the king of the crawling men
And in the gutter drownèd.

'Tis impossible that I'll stand tall
Where every other, he shall crawl.

So back I'll fall to greener lands, my hands
My feet bruised from the crawl across city floor.
And under the earth where grasping hand tore
They dragged me in the sands.

In my flight I forgot not Judgment Day
Where the crawling king crawls forever more
Punished endlessly in endless grey
As concrete compounds grow through the floor.

I was a fool who thought to cry
Was an end to innocence and manhood.
For all the sickness I beg to bring,
I'd withdraw that curse of crawling sin.

Not yet the winter of our discontent
Long is the time the crawling king repents.

Requiem

A.W.

This: the darkest hour
But it was you who, darkly inched,
Took a mile long leap,
Beyond what was condoned
It is you, I fear,
Will go back to black—
Back to the tormented night
Which drove you on.
If morning awaited you
Could you rise and walk?
From your soiled bed
To where I went
And wandered lost
But found my track.

What a brute sight,
Of packed bags and broken plates
In the broad daylight.

The stuff of the night
Brought to the unquiet mind of late,
Given fresh form in our plight:

When did our bedsheets cool
From another's heat inside,
After you'd taken it all?

What you were is a fool,
A cheat, a child trying to hide
The act of the curtain call.

'Yes' can be the worst of words for the worst of acts
Wherein our home is a bordello now
And you a whore for a coffee and a chat.

What serpents have risen in my heart!
Where I wish to blind and injure
And burn down
All matter and manna
Of us together.
And I wish that forked tongued death
Render us cthonically on perdition's dark walls.

What trinkets I keep in my crippled heart!
A line of 'ifs' and shrunken heads
That grimace back
At my eternal absence from my station
And I wish loathsome regret
Would leave my side and let me rest.

But I forgive (for I must and)
You alone are mine to forgive
For this transgression of our home.
Sometimes I fear the bottle will blind me,
Sometimes I fear myself trapped in time
Rolling around eternally.
The wounds are fresh and oozing,
And as ugly as your lying tongue and open cunt.

Still, you are not what I said you were
But what I once saw;
So if you are done and down,
And low on the ground,
I will love you like you need to be loved.
I hope you are
But doubt is strong
And I was not born to save you
But to love your best
So tread with continued care and come back.

A Thank You

Dear Reader,

I want to thank you kindly for taking the time to read this book. Whether it was purchased, borrowed or attained though other means. My main aim is to share the ideas that come through me with the world. By reading and recommending this, we begin a dialogue of profound importance.

To help me share this, I have a favour to ask of you. I would love for you to review this work on a relevant platform, such as Amazon. Recommend it, tell your friends. Leave me a message on Social Media. All of this helps more people to find and see this work. Furthermore, if you wish to pledge any further support, because you like these words, you can visit *williamcooke.net* to do just that. Every word you read of mine, every email with feedback I recieve from you is of great value to me. Every penny you pledge let's me know my work is on the right path. So I have you, my dear reader, to thank for this opportunity to pursue and grow with my craft.
I hope you understand what that means to me.

William

About The Author

Hailing from England, *William Cooke* is a Poet, Essayist, and Storyteller. He retains a profound interest in Modern and Classical tales, including Mythology. His highest purpose is to raise the profile of Mythological thought in our spiritually hungry world via recounting the secrets from his many adventures and misadventures.

Influenced by Jungian Psychology and Existential Philosophy, his main aims are to explore the eternal human experience and bring it into order. This project is a life's work and is channelled through his writings.

www.ingramcontent.com/pod-product-compliance
Lightning Source LLC
LaVergne TN
LVHW052111160826
845678LV00015B/3481

* 9 7 8 1 9 9 9 3 7 1 5 3 1 *